Dr. HOQ
I know everything
is going to be OK :)
My Prayers are with
you. I will see you when
you come back in April
Take Care
Patzy

# Inspirational
# Meditations

First published by Parragon in 2011

Parragon
Queen Street House
4 Queen Street
Bath BA1 1HE, UK

Copyright © Parragon Books Ltd 2011
Design by Pink Creative Ltd

ISBN: 978-1-4454-3848-1

Printed in China

# Inspirational
## Meditations

a collection of inspirational thoughts and images

Bath • New York • Singapore • Hong Kong • Cologne • Delhi
Melbourne • Amsterdam • Johannesburg • Auckland • Shenzhen

All it takes is one bloom of hope to make a spiritual garden.

Terri Guillemets

I will love the light for it shows me the way. Yet I will endure the darkness for it shows me the stars.

Og Mandino

It is not because things are difficult that we do not dare, it is because we do not dare that they are difficult.

Seneca

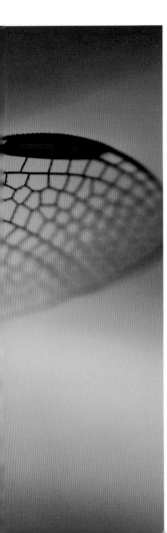

Beauty and grace
command the world.

Park Benjamin

Simplicity is making the journey of this life with just baggage enough.

Anonymous

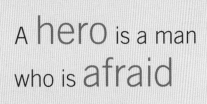

A **hero** is a man who is **afraid** to run away.

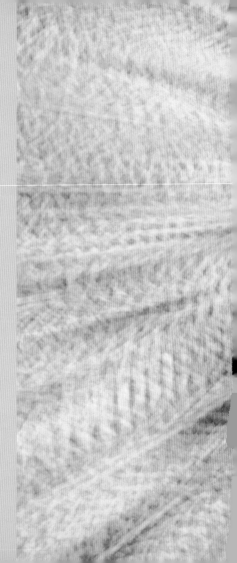

If I have seen further, it is by standing on the shoulders of giants.

Isaac Newton

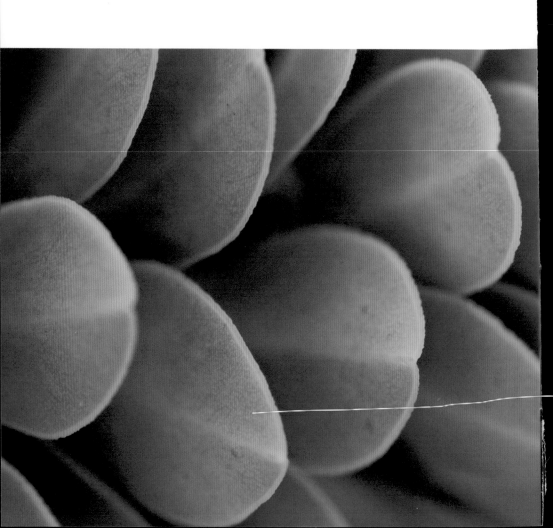

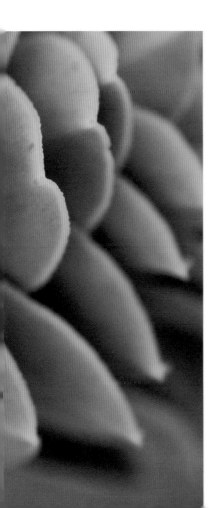

Our sorrows and wounds are healed only when we touch them with compassion.

Buddha

# Gratitude

is not only the
greatest of virtues,
but the parent
of all the others.

Cicero

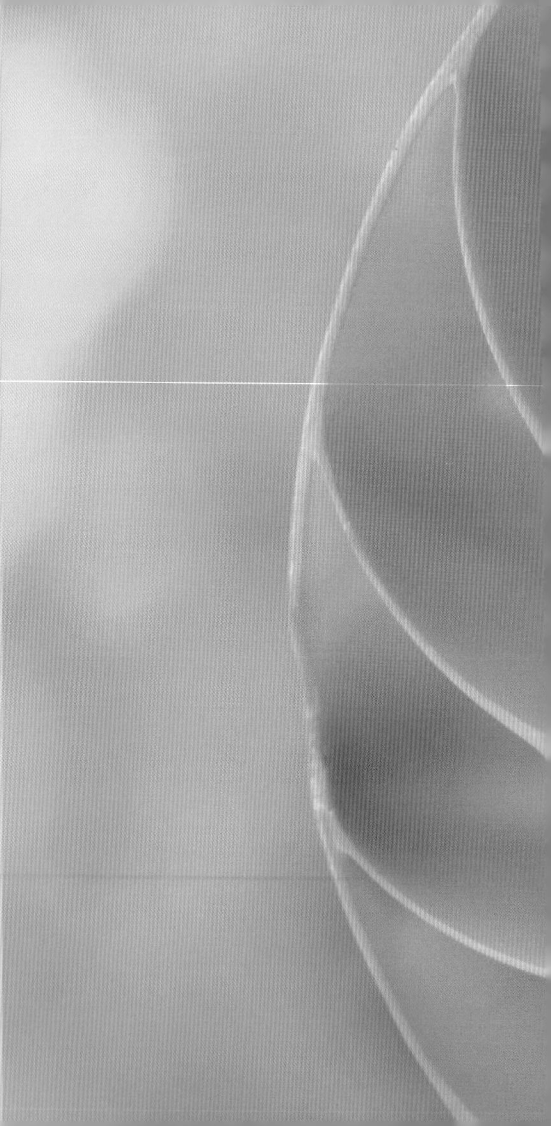

No trumpets sound when the important

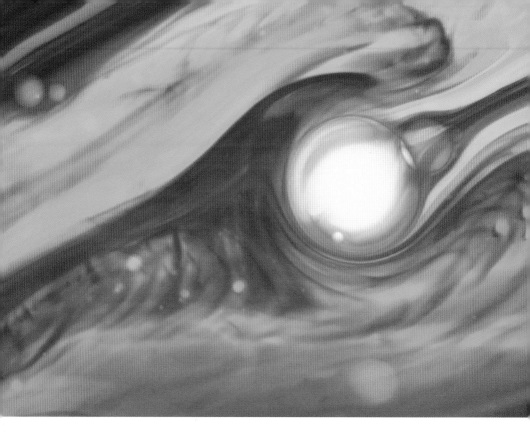

decisions of our life are made.

Destiny is made known silently.

The great thing in this world is not so much where we are, but in what direction we are moving.

Oliver Wendell Holmes

If you have
knowledge,
let others light
their candles in it.

Margaret Fuller

The real voyage of discovery consists not in seeking new landscapes, but in having new eyes.

Marcel Proust

Nothing is predestined:
The obstacles of your past
can become the gateways
that lead to new beginnings.

Ralph Blum

This above all:

to thine own self be true.

William Shakespeare

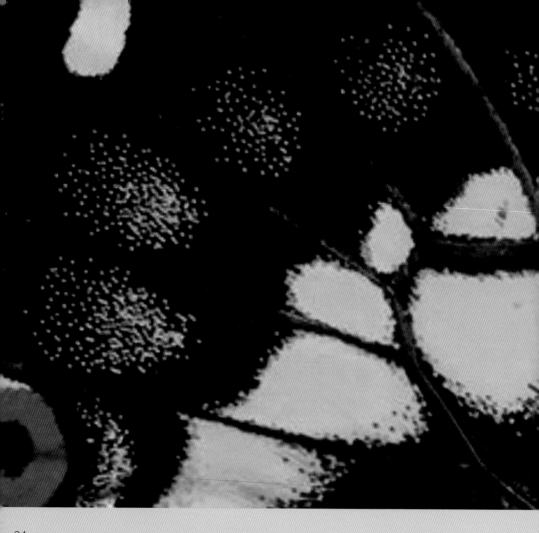

We must become
the change
we want to see.

Mahatma Gandhi

The best way to
prepare for life
is to begin to live.

Elbert Hubbard

If you could get
up the courage
to begin, you have the
courage to succeed.

David Viscott

True strength lies in submission which permits one to dedicate his life, through devotion, to something beyond himself.

Arthur Miller

Better a diamond
with a flaw than a
pebble without.

Confucius

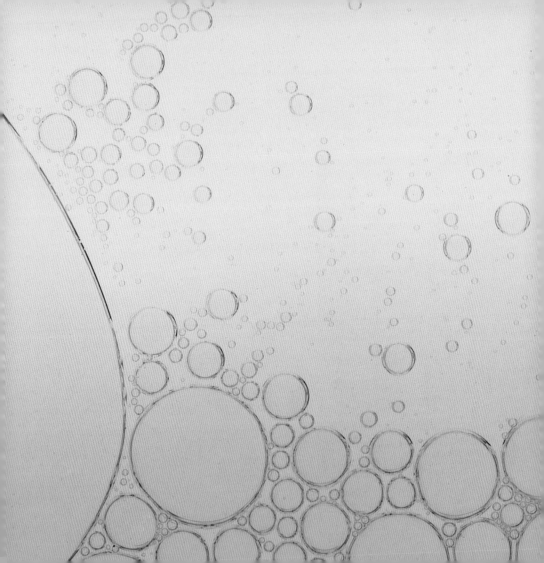

Courage is the discovery that you may not win, and trying when you know you can lose.

Tom Krause

All misfortune is but a stepping stone to fortune.

Henry David Thoreau

Take rest; a field that has rested gives a bountiful crop.

Ovid

51

# Confidence
is half of victory.

Yiddish Proverb

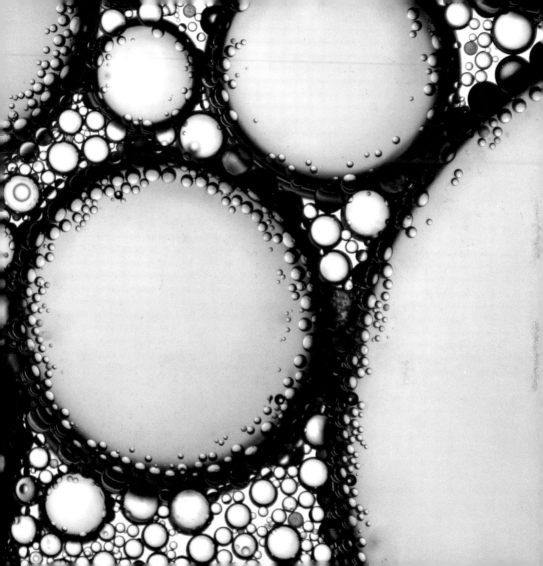

Success is the good fortune that comes from aspiration, desperation, perspiration and inspiration.

Evan Esar

Better to light a candle than to curse the darkness.

Chinese Proverb

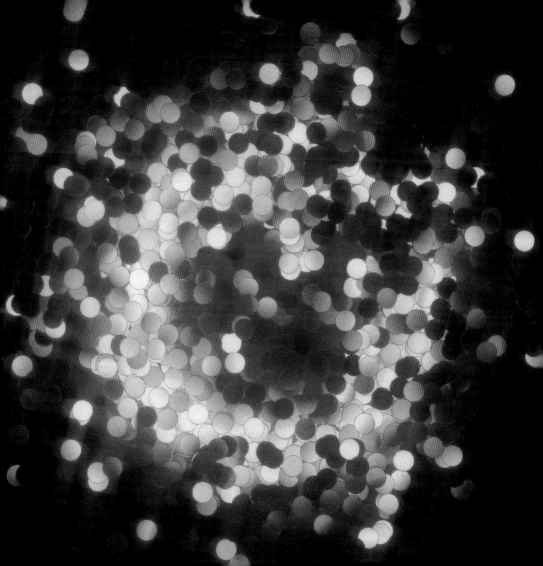

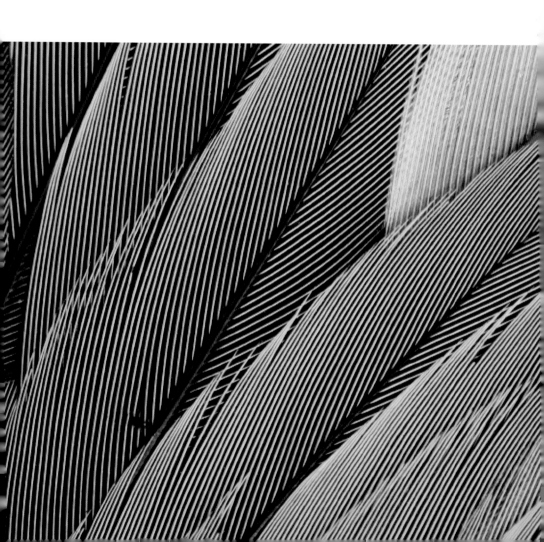

# Knowing

yourself is the

beginning of all

# wisdom.

Aristotle

Life isn't about
finding yourself.
Life is about
creating yourself.

George Bernard Shaw

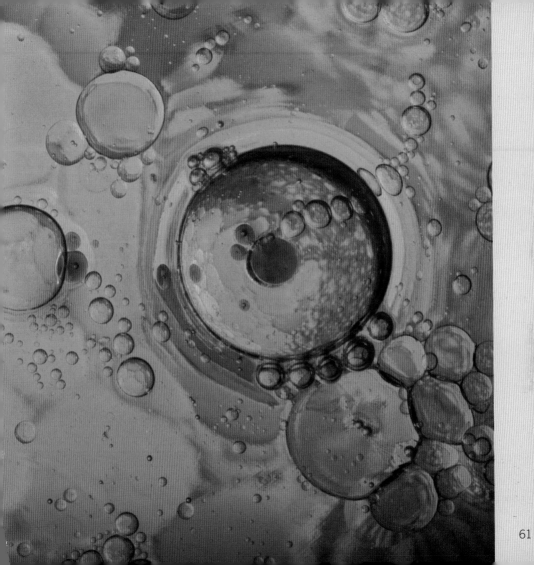

Don't let what you can't do stop you from doing what you can do.

John Wooden

The best
motivation
always comes
from within.

Michael Johnson

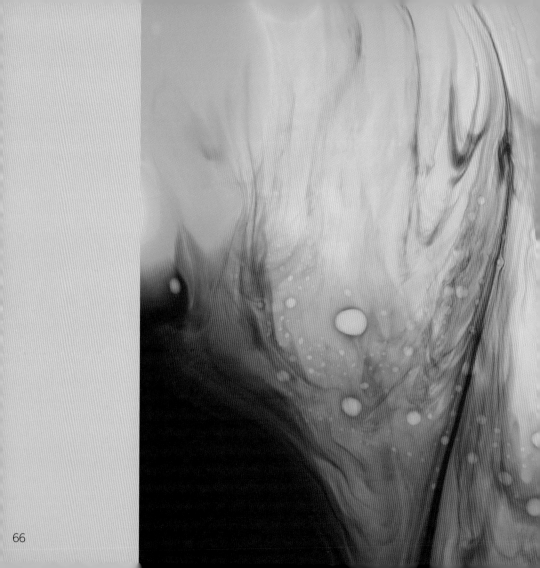

The only journey
is the journey within.

Rainer Maria Rilke

I want to be all
that I am capable of
becoming.

Katherine Mansfield

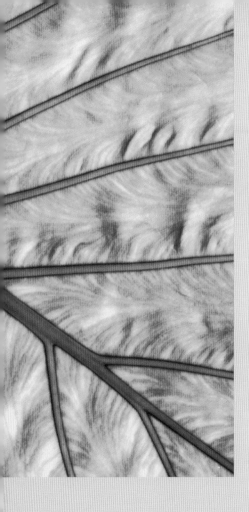

The true meaning of life is to plant trees, under whose shade you do not expect to sit.

Nelson Henderson

Collect as precious pearls
the words of the wise
and virtuous.

Abd-el-Kadar

He that will not reflect is a ruined man.

Asian Proverb

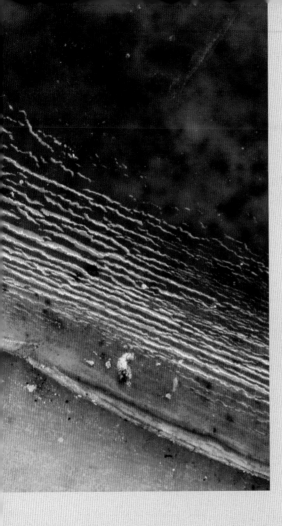

# Happiness
is not a station
you arrive at,
but a manner
of traveling.

Margaret Runbeck

Life is not meant to be easy, my child; but take courage — it can be delightful.

George Bernard Shaw

Patience, persistence
and perspiration make
an unbeatable
combination for
success.

Napoleon Hill

The world **breaks** everyone, and afterward many are **strong** in the broken places.

Ernest Hemingway

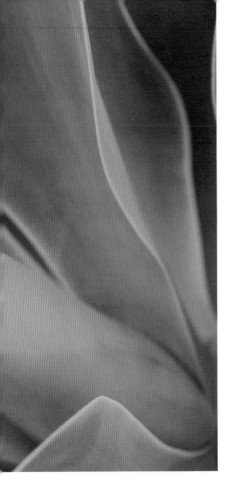

No law or ordinance
is mightier than
understanding.

Plato

Really great people make you feel that you, too, can become great.

Mark Twain

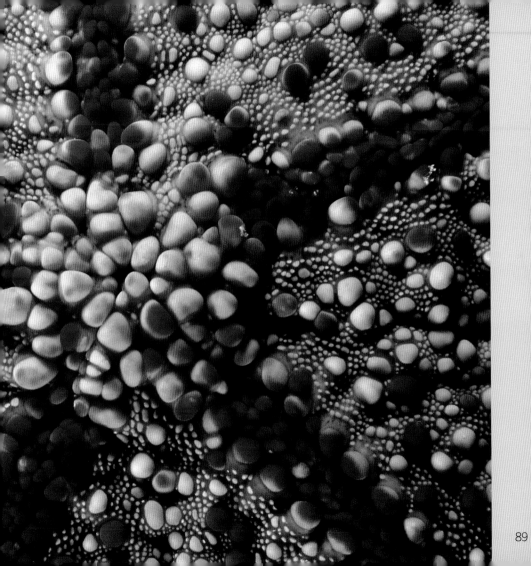

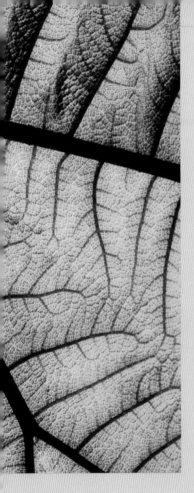

The highest reward
for a person's toil is not
what they get for it, but what
they become by it.

John Ruskin

When I let go
of what I am,
of what I am,
I become what
I might be.

Lao Tzu

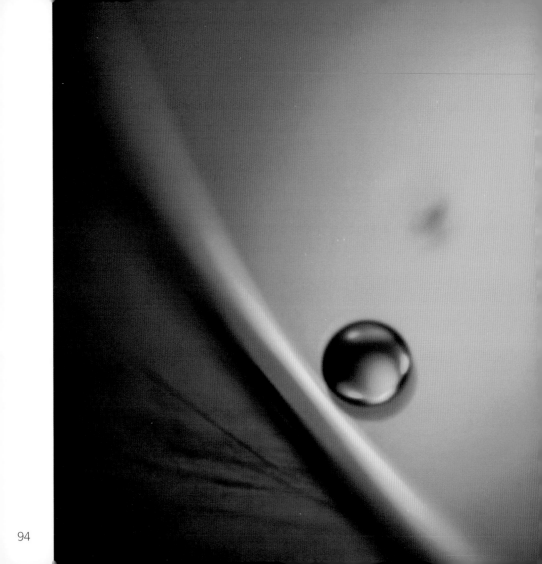